WHAT WE'VE BECOME

poems by

darlene anita scott

Finishing Line Press
Georgetown, Kentucky

WHAT WE'VE BECOME

ACKNOWLEDGMENTS

A Series of Misunderstandings, *Green Mountains Review*
Weekday, 4 a.m., *Warpland*
The Spirit, *Warpland*
How Tomorrow Might Look, *Zaira*
Things I Must Remember, *Pen + Brush*
So the Snapshots Say, *Family Pictures*
Rash in the Shape of My Locs, *Pen + Brush*
Oral Myology, Or How to Know When It's Over, *MadCap Review*
Once the Girls Are Drunk on Rice Wine, *Proud To Be*
Too Beautiful A Day To Die, *Awakenings Review*
My Vivid Imagination Paint You, Instead, Grey, *Star 82 Review*

Publisher: Leah Huete de Maines
Editor: Christen Kincaid
Cover Art: Courtesy of Author
Author Photo: Lechele Jackson
Cover Design: Elizabeth Maines McCleavy

Order online: www.finishinglinepress.com
also available on amazon.com

Author inquiries and mail orders:
Finishing Line Press
PO Box 1626
Georgetown, Kentucky 40324
USA

Contents

for Mommy & Daddy: Gloria A. & Ernest H. Scott Jr.

"You who mattered me into being."
Lauren K. Alleyne

A SERIES OF MISUNDERSTANDINGS

About blood: it's only one means of being alive.
Every living cognitive doesn't have or use it
to transport nutrients & oxygen. Sometimes
creatures use alternative systems. This means
there are ways of being alive that look nothing
like the somatic supposition opposite death.

To be dead is something else altogether. Blood
is not always red. Sometimes, in these othered
living cognitives it is blue. Like in some species
of octopus. Which is to say that blue blood is
not the antithesis to the lowly regular'ed *red blood*
*& blue bloo*d is not ascendant. Nor should it be.

First blood announces a girl body's readiness
to make more bodies, except when it's not. This
is when blood is shed from her womb, zealous as
a changing tide, since there is no need to shuttle
nutrients & oxygen. Other mammals absorb the
unused tissue which is, apparently, another way

of bleeding. For dogs who release at least something
ferrous & in intervals, the primitive longing
that prompts the discharge may happen twice a year.
A lioness in estrous may fulfill her need over 100 times
a day with multiple partners at approximate intervals
of 17 minutes. Which may mean loving & being loved

can feel nothing or exactly like need.

KWANSABA IN WHICH YOU STAY

I am a puddle you stomp clumsy
or playful; absorb & ombre into stain.
Dampen the anodyne bass of blood flow
warm with kinetic traffic of oxygen &
what once was. Caress of curious healers:
hands slick with my thin wet. You.
Never riled by the sight of blood.

WHAT WE'VE BECOME

On the 13465th time,
the faces above the mantel tsk us.
We turn our backs to them; make
mental notes to rearrange next
Saturday, our to-do-list day, but
not this day, Sunday, when we
go lazy & practice what this
should feel like on Mondays,
Wednesdays, Tuesdays, just
as the week creeps to its close
on Thursdays, or when we're
tired on Fridays falling into sleep
after take-out boxes of garlicky
string beans, wine, marinated tofu.
We are the ones we always wanted
yet never expected to be. Their glares
incite no blushes from us: Here? Now?
Is it me or you who moans an affirmative
that has nothing to do with their queries?
If we stay lucky, will always mean we are
who we wanted & never expected to be.
On any given day, years in, that ends in Y,
as passionate & patient as we were the first time.

WEEKDAY, 4 A.M.

We start the day
before the day
by making love.

We welcome dawn
with orange juice
and newsworthy news;
traffic reports and r&b.

We replace pajamas
with our uniforms—
plastic smiles and steel nerves.

Disrobe carelessly
but not mindlessly.
There is still some mystery there.

We pray quickly at the door:
May the lord watch between us.
When we're apart
we manage well.

At the close of dangerous days
of daring to walk without shuffling,
hold our heads shoulder level,
we rescue each other in hugs.

Believe in our love
the way history tells us
we shouldn't.

We laugh.
Sometimes we grind
until long after the last song.

We have disagreed,
have disappointed,
have shouted and cried.
Slept on opposite sides of the bed.
Told friends of clandestine passion marks,
broken furniture, why we never pressed charges:
secrets we should've kept to ourselves.

Today we start the day
before the day
by making love.
Welcome dawn
with orange juice
and newsworthy news;
traffic reports and r&b.

And we will manage well.

URGE

Possession is the condition
that baptizes ankles feathers
in anticipation of flight.
As if the ground beneath is fire.

Honied danger, anodyne thrill.
Possession is the condition.
Breech-anxious, furious fit of birth
advent so cruel the body breaks.

The body multiplies water
& denies it release.
Possession is the condition:
brine & nine tenths any reason.

Body swells lifting heat to praise.
Numbing the feet under its weight,
breaching the walls in a ring shout
Possession is the condition.

THE SPIRIT

I.
The strings of syllables didn't belong together
according to Mrs. Fountain's phonics lessons.
Consonants piled thick as July heat; vowels only
suggested.

A heavy leather covered Bible played desk-top
to my eight-year-old doodles until something-
like words.

II.
Promises always come with return receipts in case
something doesn't fit; in case funds are insufficient;
if there is no real need for them. So I don't buy them.

Not high-hats brushed like whispers; husky as the just
before, right after voice. Strings of syllables, barely even
a suggestion of vowels.

III.
I'm eight again.
Mouth crowded with
my own something-like
words. So close to god
as birth, death, & you.

THINGS WE BLAME OUR MOUTHS FOR

We are breaking like lips ready to be kissed.
Even if my follicles pox at every place
you touch, even gilded plaster of Paris powders
in time. Something thicker than humidity
limbers our words, ropes we twist into
every time. But let's blame Him.

He promised to leave yet didn't. Left
soy sauce from steak he overcooked.
In one journal is flush plus more
than initials. But your proof is
where you imagined stains—
bleached so as approximate
as real.

Let your tongue clap against the syllables, a fury.
I stomp them for miles most mornings;
sniffling them to the back of my throat,
flinging them against unwitting brush;
have wrung what I could from shirts.
He was not in those bushes;
is not any wet you wonder.

HOW TOMORROW MIGHT LOOK

We are at war.
Imagine our lunch splattering
against the cacophony, tomatoes
turned sauce & stain. Imagine the floors
now shanks of wood we chance for retreat.
Imagine our lips baring teeth, white flags
misunderstood. Imagine the linens,
twisted as winding sheets, unsterile
gauze. Imagine this bed:
the DMZ.

STEEL DRUM

He watched his body from across the room.
Sweat mazed through tight curls in the small
of his back soaking the waistband of his shorts.

Watching himself dreaming mango & dominoes,
blasé beer, women in thin dresses that silhouette
their asses; draw them dimpled like steel drums,

he knew there were a million ways he could have said
it but he chose: "Turn to me." Plum nails of the hand

he reached for stabbed eagerly. Her entire body was
steel, his words mallets words tapping the old songs.

AFTER YEARS OF DAUGHTERS

He refuses creamed corn, will not touch broccoli
& barely fingertips the rail edging the ramp. So
the girls let him be when he exhausts himself by
existing. The TV reflects off his boots; its canned
laughter replaces his. His hands hold his abdomen;
hands that midwifed batteries from hot rod aspirants
he knew would likely live & die perched on cinder
blocks as if ready to take flight. Money he made wore
smudges of his oily thumbs like kisses for the girls,
now women, he loved.

THINGS I MUST REMEMBER

How [often] to polish the silver.
To remove eggs from the refrigerator
in advance & always level the sugar
& flour. That tomatoes are best in
summer, raw—with plenty of salt.

Proper application of the word "dear;"
Mercurochrome works for any ailment;
& only Dove will do. Never abbreviate
names except in anger—abbreviation is
not an endearment. It is diminishing or
worse, lazy.

To read for information; entertainment
is relative. To give it a chance. Refuse or
resist. Always eat something to break
the fast. & of course, something salty
with your sweets (once at dinner & again
before bed). To wear an apron & a slip.

Land is worth more than the structure on it;
to invest in the earth. How long to boil fudge
before it seizes. What seizing looks like.

The impermanence of things.
To send cards. To save cards.
That easy words are best left
to cards; hard ones ride on
spit or empty air.

SO THE SNAPSHOTS SAY

They had their moments: the two
of them afro to afro at a roadside
stop, on Aunt Edna's couch, spell-
bound beneath & by each other's
Afro-Sheened halos ridged like the
nanoscale edges on the surface
of flowers that meddle with light
so that their nectar can be located
most efficiently.

His lips pursed over Kool cigarettes.
Him belting the lyrics of *Cool Jerk*
& 45s they played after Sunday supper.
Hers parted in deliberation as they play
Scrabble & gin rummy in the den.

Weekday dinners & birthday parties.
In communion around the Formica table
over a meal curated with the appropriate
flavor of Kool-Aid. Breaking bread over
the oil bill, whose teacher had called in
a mischief report.

Afros braided down, kids full & tucked
like the tally of silver & gold anniversaries
whose shadows always ruin the shot. You
are subjects without a proper light source,
eyes vapid & unfocused. Your blush not
so bright when the shudders are off.
Did you try to adjust the settings?

THE SCIENCE OF SIDEWALKS

For the sidewalk in front of my childhood home

One theory says they exist to shelter
tree roots that itch in our lips—
swelled notices of who we belong to.
Are wayward rallies of knee peeling crumbs
that no storm can disrupt or scatter.
Like how we gather our broken, lay
warm cover to protect them through winter.

RASH IN THE SHAPE OF MY LOCS

I'm careless with the food;
it burns. You're too hungry
to notice it happens every time.

Always so hungry that I don't
concentrate on the food only
the feeding, so it burns every
time: palimpsest of our history
plated on white stoneware. We
have never made love the same
way twice unless you count the
hunger.

Sometimes in dementia, five minutes
& five hours can feel the same.

My aunt cautioned me routine
is a weapon. Maybe like a fork
can stab or feed. But we use our
hands where conversations could
be. Our words are skittish brakes
that never warn exhaustion
(if we engage them at all). We are
heedless to any potential injury
unless you count our choice to use
hands.

Sometimes in dementia even
the organs forget what to do.

In spring birds nest in our soffits.
They announce their hunger
so loud they subjugate the TV &
like first world emergencies: heed,
empathy, & appropriate timbre.

Rage against the newly alive things
transports cement in place of blood
through the capillaries in my head.

Sometimes in dementia,
brain cells adopt new roles.

I'm careless with my weight; rest my head
against your arm until it's limp & damp,
pocked in a rash in the shape of my locs.

Sometimes in dementia familiar environs
can become prisons, mazes, a womb.

AS IF EVERY SONG IS THE FIRST WE MADE LOVE TO

You tasted baby-after-sleep sour—saccharine & tart;
lukewarm in my hairline damp & dancing in the no-
rush of a ride through the city for ice pops & discards.

Your voice measured rim shot to snare tap after we
talked too long, your neck an arch over my knee, eyes
fissures I had to ooze my way into 'til you were every bit

the shimmer of a high hat. My sweat evaporated just beneath
follicles, no chill to be named. Like the break between timpani
& the next plea, a lyric too ardent to hear. I could stop denying

my ears; let my feet choose. You could invent more subtle ways
to enter a body. Say anything: cilia plays coy, shimmies from
the tickle. Belly hollows into an echo that fits the whole of us.

ORAL MYOLOGY, OR HOW TO KNOW IT'S OVER

How It crowds space, can be music;
too much: cacophony. Erodes enamel
diluting to anemia all intentions.

How it offers words when we want ears,
to scream, invading tongue. To swallow it
or mud. As apology with intestines empty

of anything like sorry; distended malnourished
belly tattletaling the empty offering. Have you
ever offered your tongue as alms like the blue

of sky everlasting yet knowing elsewhere
it's pink-purple or grey or black as bile,
necessarily rancid to digest what's left after the chew?

BY THE END OF THE STORY SOMEONE MUST DIE

We talk nearly all night until
she offers *Go to sleep; I can tell*
you're tired. I am. Cold tangle of
nerves for her nimble fingers.

In the melting of my caution
I am an assault of snores cornered
in her arms. Something must be
required of the f.o.i.l. other than
watching, waxing, waiting. Gift
her patience before leaving
unnaturally tired as if sleep
never happened. She haggles:
toast & chocolate milk. I know

better; even the dew is ice. My lips
crack as soon as I'm on the other
side of the door; pick-up basketball
& an empty stomach on deck.

ONCE THE BAR-GIRLS ARE DRUNK ON RICE WINE

We smudge with Kools & Camels, expel
our demons to vapor, crowding the bar like
rashes   pebbling our skin.

In the heft of damp BDUs, the lingering incense
blesses this temple   of unfamiliar.

Pour more liquor; satisfy Empty long enough
to carry us   through cycles we name Rest.
In between: pencil sketches & wobbly

lyrics ride lines home. What becomes of the broken-
hearted: Out of tune & touch
                                         with our imminent deaths.

The girls are more bone
than heat. Come   with velocity
if not volume. We drain

into gutters of them & of streets.
Salt the earth   with bravado
foreign soil lapping our progeny.

We swim   with closed eyes.
Reckless for orders
we are compelled to commit,

repeat & forget.
Somewhere guilt is thin & late
for the season. A merry Christmas

it won't be. Back home our girls set
the ice cream on the counter to soften
the fear   in their chests.

MY VIVID IMAGINATION PAINTS YOU, INSTEAD, GREY

Your breath in the morning—sour milk like a baby we knew
would never happen but dreamt library cards & the grandparents
our parents would be. The knobs of your wrists girdled by brushed
steel you couldn't get on or off without me that dangles elegantly
yet wide enough to compel me to return instead of sell when it fell
behind my bathroom door.
(You didn't notice).

I had no other way to say goodbye.

Whenever we did, there were your fingers—each taking its own time
to release my back, hip, the hem of my top—to vices that would
recast whatever seemed right into something better; as forbidden.
Creased skin between your eyebrows grooves I got lost in.
Lines for, clearly of, telling.

Except we erased each story
to make room for cheaper metaphors.

I still chase the mutinous curls attempting a clean getaway
from your shot at taming, meandering down your neck
from one of the bands I found, later, between the couch cushions;
gather your pieces yet the puzzle is no less complicated. We never
gave why any credit; wolf of our longing prickly insistent
sand between our wet toes.

Suddenly I miss you like you're dead.

TOO BEAUTIFUL A DAY TO DIE
After Albert Camus

Sometimes it's 12:37 and you press the dark
to your eyelids. Crush your knees into your
chest. You honor the hour's invitation, spec-
ulative fingers strumming diffidence like you
don't know better. Someone has to make the

music. *The body resists annihilation.* Have you
ever seen a chicken decapitated? Crossed the
Potomac on the Nice Memorial Bridge with-
out both hands knuckle white until Maryland?
4:30 indecision is study & practice. Or, you tell

the Suicide Line attendant you just want to talk.
Claim no one & let him offer: 911, your Job,
Church, the Kids. Even your Paycheck. *So where
is this call center located? Do you prefer white? Or wheat?*
In the not-so-South South this October Sunday

you stall: *my body is breaking and needs epoxy.*
You confide human hands fail their grip. That
you also tried to shrink. And expand. With dis-
appointing results. Both tasted like expedience
and moss; burned the tongue with sun. Which

is to wonder how rainy days earn such a bad rap.
It's too beautiful a day to die. A different 4:30 and
more than many pills divvied over hours have made
your waste black, headaches they're supposed to
extinguish and you're satisfied: control. Upstairs

bathroom assimilates all of it: confessional and storage.
5:43 you retreat into his insistence *Good morning to you
too.* Frost is regalia over the city. Y'all quickly make
something you will record as love while he's at work.
Collect its ashes, gargle and discard in the sink. He's
watching yet you dare scan your eyes for sun.

BENEDICTION

A mother buries her second son
after taking the crumbs of his body
from some unholy place in the secret
of night—car lights replaced by shadows
she slips into. Crunching candy wrappers
underfoot remind her of the crowd jeering
for souvenirs of his flesh. Her heart races ahead.

Crickets lullaby; she doesn't sleep. She moves steadily
through years on top of more years of life believing in god.

That's how I believe in you.

The way it takes sunshine to make shadows,
how it defies even rain some summer evenings;
the way, they say, the devil beats his wife
& how its scent is never captured
in incense & candles
bearing its name.

I invoke you without trying.

A lone feather floats as if possessed
while I hum to the twenty third Psalm
sung over a Nyabinghi drum today. You are.
The pink of my palm and I need you as much.

OUTSIDE CLOTHES

The alibi wasn't the one they wanted.
On me he tries headache, long day
at the yard, shit on his mind—a list
of grievances to distance us in a bed
I used not be able to find a spot
his arms were not.

I search his back, his shoulder blade
shudders and the only light is sheen
of his sweat. Press my nose into the
shadow. Many have been lost in dark
as dangerous as any alley shortcut;
colder than lead of berettas or batons.

He's so stiff I'm almost convinced
I've lost him. Hold my breath, save
it for him, catch his trembles until
they release him in a puddle of stories
we tuck away with the others this bed
could—but won't—ever tell.

darlene anita scott is a writer and multidisciplinary artist who explores corporeal presentations of trauma and the violence of silence especially for Black girls. She has exhibited her artwork on the "good girl" widely. Her publications include the poetry collection *Marrow* (University Press of Kentucky) and an edited creative/critical volume *Revisiting the Elegy in the Black Lives Matter Era* (Routledge).